Introduction

Yoga, which has its origins in the Hindu East, is conscious union with your divine center; it is internal order, an end to the dominating aspect of the mind, a merging with the whole, a transcendence of the partial.

BUDHI is our intellect, or prism for seeing things. The line that unites mind and heart.

The path of the union of our intellect with the source is called YOGA BUDHI. Indeed, pure conscious consciousness is the origin of all manifestations. This, then, is the yoga of conscious consciousness. "SAMATHA BUDHI" is the balanced mind that overcomes and transforms "SANGHA BUDHI," or the associative mind.

The combination of YOGA (union) with KARMA (action) produces KARMA YOGA, where every action is performed as an offering of love to the ONE GOD with no attachment to any outcome.

There are many types of yoga, such as:

BAHKTI: The yoga of return to the ONE GOD. It is love for love's sake; a genuine devotee thus does not need anything else.

HATHA: The yoga of ASANAS, or psycho-physical positions for integration, health and stability. This yoga includes the Mudras.

KUNDALINI: The yoga of SHAKTI, or energetic force that lodges at the base of the spine, and its awakening and ascent through the 7 archetypal chakras.

RAJA: The yoga of the mind and its movement, to develop conscious alertness.

JNANA: The yoga of inquiry, to cultivate wisdom.

PRANAYAMA: The yoga of vitality, which teaches the stabilization of breath in order to suppress thought.

Yoga integrates ANTAKHARANA as an internal instrument of development in order to disintegrate external antagonisms. Whoever practices yoga must be conscious of the unity of TRIKARMA:

- ❖ Thought: as the making of a decision

- ❖ Words: as the expression of the decision

- ❖ Action: as the implementation of the decision

We refer to this coordination of thought-words-deeds as the harmonization of the three manifestations of the human personality.

All this leads to DHARMA, or the individual's duty to find the ONE GOD within himself as a divine spark. If found, the conflicts in our inclinations disappear. When your actions are filled with DHARMA, you are on your way to realizing BRAHMAN, the indivisible absolute. The authentic divinity. If you recognize DHARMA you discover that the Supreme Being "the ONE GOD" is the essence, and that we are instruments of divinity in action.

"The Practitioner's Prayer"

Oh child of Yoga,
The fate of each incarnation is to
achieve conscious consciousness of
infinite love.
Love is the only way, the one
true path to the Realization of
God in Ourselves. Love is
purity, Unity and divinity,
beyond past and future.

YUG- means union.
YOGA- means unity.

YOGI- is one that recognizes conscious unity.

The Individual

The individual is an IMAGE.

- ❖ Physical body

- ❖ Individual consciousness

- ❖ Waking world

They are all linked; and behind it all is primordial and infinite conscious consciousness, and the only absolute reality, our true "I."

All this means that whatever categories one may fit into personally, whether father, mother, son, daughter, brother, sister, grandfather, uncle, husband, cousin, etc. go no further than the individual.

As long as you are engaged with the individual image you will look outward without inquiring inward; this is why ignorance of one's real identity (Aham) is known as fundamental ignorance. The body-mind complex is also called the Illusory "I," manifesting a feeling that one is a doer, with no consideration given to causation.

In fundamental ignorance, and under the sway of this feeling, individual images seek to secure and control everything they think is THEIRS, from the limited perspective of their thought. Under that illusion, they have never realized that their whole life has been about fear of material loss, based on a false individual feeling corresponding to a "ME" and a "MINE" with no us, coupled with cunning, calculation and speculation.

The individual's projection as an image thus experiences a feeling of separation, and directs itself toward structures and towards maintaining the status quo of the structure "at any cost"; this state, however, lacks all innocence, because the mind divided by its own interest sees only dangers around it.

We will also refer to this individual or image as the conditioned "I," but each individual has an invisible basis: the true "I," which in the teachings is known as ATMA, or reality beyond appearances whereas the conditioned "I" is "asleep" relative to conscious consciousness. In this world of temporal objects, life seems to work in "Opposites" because the individual mind sees "Two Sides."

This duality of the individual mind attached to the Sensory Senses and the physical body is what maintains the illusory identification with "names and forms." The five sensory senses are like sensors:

❖ The visual sense / SEEING

❖ The auditory sense / HEARING

❖ The olfactory sense / SMELL

❖ The tactile sense / TOUCH

❖ The vocal sense / TASTE

These five functional senses are always deceptive, but this sensory deception is not grasped by the individual "I," conditioning and binding to the mind and body. The deception of the senses is such that they make human beings feel that the earth is stationary; yet we know that this is not so. Our earthly globe moves like a spinning top seeking to "rest," or to stop its dancing; in fact, that movement forces its axis to trace out a circumference in space that manifests what we refer to as the precession of the equinoxes.

Our earthly globe is alive, but the five sensory senses are like the trick of the game, because they SIMULATE STATES.

A deep understanding of this simulation gives rise to the insight that perception can be conditioned by creating an image of reality. The individual, however, confuses the image with the reality; in other words, he IDEALIZES, while reality ENDURES.

The omnipresent ONE GOD is unchanging in its conscious center.

In the nexus of mind, body and senses, it is the mind that projects "two sides" so as to be able to codify its communication; it is reflected beyond the moment of conscious consciousness itself. When you are fully conscious, you come to grasp sensory deception, and your moderation and inviolability emerge as social practice. And the mouth is the door, because it is through the mouth that you speak and eat.

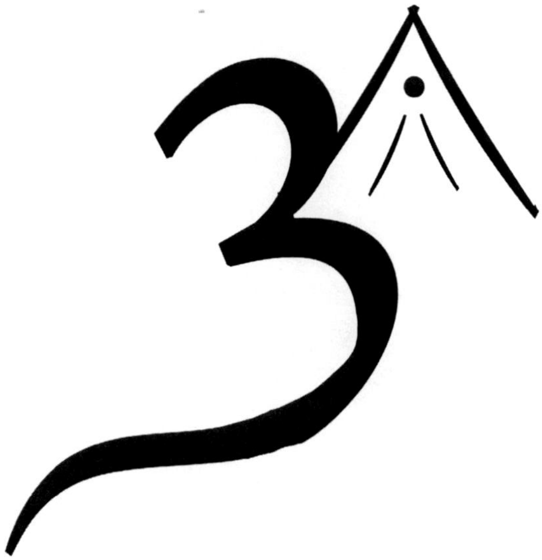

Actual Renunciation

In Yoga BUDHI, Actual Renunciation consists in realizing that you are not the body into which cause and effect ultimately flow; only then can you understand that consciousness is not a function of the mind, concentrated in the physical brain in your body: consciousness is INFINITE, UNIVERSAL and ETERNAL. Consciousness is our true "I," which manifested both the mind and the cosmos without the substrate undergoing any change. It is beyond time and is not affected by the physical death of the temporal body.

Human beings of both genders and their individual personalities present as follows:

- ❖ The dense physical body (vehicular)

- ❖ The subtle body (because the individual mind creates its own world of imaginary forms and experiences in its wishful dreaming)

- ❖ The fortuitous body (which guards the ideal), if human beings fail to understand their cause, neither can they assimilate their effect.

Consciously knowing (that you are not your body) allows you to transcend the personal, that part in you that asserts its separateness. Without any consciousness of this Actual Renunciation, you push yourself towards an illusory projection of the world as a stage-play of the divided mind, which we will call the Movement.

If you identify with your body, which is not you, your own identity disappears - what you really are. And so, you become attached:

❖ To the individual mind: Duality and the Past

❖ To the 5 sensory senses: Deception

IDENTIFICATION is your "Outward" gaze, reflecting you. It implies total ignorance of the "Inward" (the permanence within yourself). This mental sensory attention - outward - is broken up by the daily events that occur in the transience of time and space, which is understood as LINEAR.

Since the particular mind is disappointed by the deceiving senses, it forms opinions on each changing piece of information, over and over again; thus the individual image is affected by transience as a personality, without this transience being the blame for its various states.

First, the CONDITIONED I becomes emotionally involved with what it sees. The emotion becomes a feeling. And then, every time, this feeling generates a mood.

By this mechanism, the individual personality becomes TEMPERAMENTAL. And the peculiar thing about these events is that they are experienced from the perspective of their limitation of (beginning and end), yet cannot be avoided. Consequently, it is "The End" that is always of concern to the individual personality.

Only by becoming aware that we are not our bodies can the mystery of the (beginning and end) be brought to its conclusion.

Whatever is born must die; what is permanent in you is neither born nor dies. It is not dual, it does not transit. But the individual mind, in its limitation, is concerned only with intellectual distinctions and rational differences, based on the body and its status quo.

Each I, identified with the body as a name and a form, becomes what drives thoughts out of alignment with words and actions, because what fuels the individual mind is conditioned memory. The conditioned I embeds its references into the memory and conditions it; this is how it makes the past into its master and owner.

Thought is what PROJECTS the world of the person identified by names and forms, and when thought brings about misaligned action, the identified person expects to obtain certain results or fruits. If these results or fruits are not as expected, the two-sided mind that projected them experiences suffering, because it has not known Actual Renunciation.

With Actual Renunciation, or the knowledge that you are not your body, BUDHI - the mind able to look inward - begins to purify itself until you can successfully TAKE REFUGE.

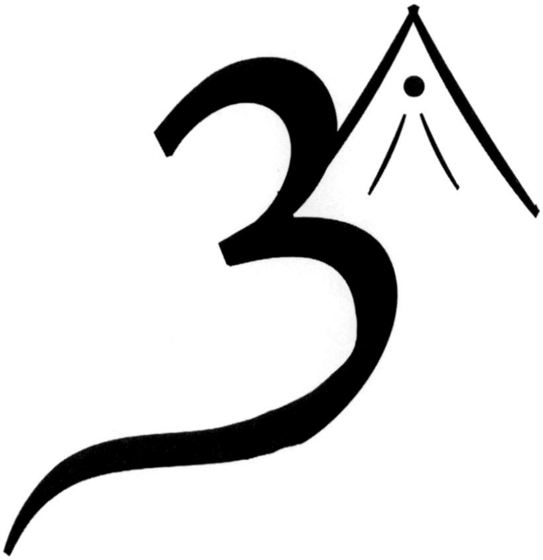

Taking Refuge

The highest purpose of BUDHI as mind-intellect is TAKING REFUGE, as PURE DISCERNMENT.

BUDHI is mind with the ability to discern, differentiate and intuit. Though this intellect or prism of seeing inclines towards reason, it also projects itself towards the physical body without being elevated. An immature intellect can produce intellectuals and thinkers that are great, yet are identified by name and form, and thus closed off from their own internal LIGHT.

Intellectual reason would seem to be the culmination of this world of thought projection, but it is in fact so only in APPEARANCES, because the intellect of a sleeping consciousness avails itself only of memory, with psychological attachment. Such is the world of relations, where attraction and repulsion play their role, like the individual mind projected onto the physical body is related to the sensory senses its deception is perceptual; it becomes entangled in differences of caste, religion, color, race, creed... because intellectual reason has a need to argue, question and defend a point of view.

BUDHI intellect is like our "Precious Jewel," because it can TRANSCEND to intuit and only if we develop intuition can there emerge discernment as to what is real and what is unreal.

Before you TAKE REFUGE, the JEWEL is clouded, and the conditioned "I" will chase after dense matter, burdened by the past and duality.

With the JEWEL clouded, you are a separate part, debating and antagonizing what you consider to be other (separate parts), unrelated to your thinking. While this is happening, (reality remains reality); only when BUDHI matures can you take refuge, because then YOU PERCEIVE and ACCEPT that all that is changing and transitory in the ideation of the self-ignorant mental ego is unreality; it is then that you can abandon reason and its need to argue over transitory matters. Thus you can expand the intuition that corresponds to being, and fully receive the light. A balance then emerges in the prism in which things are embellished and separate. Such is the PURE DISCERNMENT that naturally accompanies detachment.

TAKING REFUGE IN BUDHI is about (perceiving) and (accepting) that what endures in you simply "IS" and has no beginning or end. One, with no counterpart. Indestructible and inexhaustible divinity.

From the refuge of BUDHI to infinity, there is only the void, because it has become clear that BUDHI is the line that unites the mind to the heart. As this line loses luster, it needs to be cleaned. So you know that you have genuinely taken refuge when the constant, ever-elevated connection and absolute respect for divinity that transcends the mind never again departs from you. As it happens, to conceive of Pure Discernment is the great gift of the ONE to YOGA BUDHI as AMRITA, the Great Restorative Force.

He who takes refuge is like a Yogi, who has no attachment to objective matter, yet does not feel separated from it. NOW life is moment to moment, with no burden, and every moment without mind is TOTAL. In understanding YOGA BUDHI we learn that unless a individual human personality secures wisdom, unwavering devotion and spiritual firmness as an aspirant, he may be tempted to see himself as a victim of the passionate past of his ego, bestowed upon him by his own imagination.

Wisdom alone overcomes duality, because it is beyond any conditioned pattern.

The Object is as transitory as your body; identification gives rise to attachment and the struggle over rival created interests, forgetting that the ONE GOD is in every separate part. It is through identification that the mental ego experiences the feeling of separation, or the idea of the "I" as separate.

With actual renunciation and taking refuge, a person is impelled towards spiritual realization evolving into conscious consciousness, thus overcoming the fear of the end, which engenders the fear of death, as if it were not a natural act. Nature, meanwhile, is the manifestation of god. Captured by the "I" through the five sensory senses. CONSCIOUS Consciousness is what connects the changes that are manifested to the nucleous core of being. In practice, conscious consciousness means realizing what is real in this divine game of the One. Conscious consciousness is what integrates the totality as a mutual understanding, in an indivisible unity. Only spiritual consciousness can reveal the silent and permanent nucleous core, (your observer witness), which can once again become unaffected by its ETERNAL CONDITION OF PERMANENCE in the face of all transient changes. That witness is ATMA quality of being, hence conscious consciousness is the only thing that can reflect with no need to be reflected; this means that only conscious consciousness that is aware of itself can set an example of evolution, by its integrated and exemplary conduct of effortless life.

The mind cannot do this without a conscious center. The mind does not connect, it only projects illusion and objective reaction reflected in transience. Because it is in the mind that the feeling of separation arises.

The mind is only an executor of form; hence the mental ego can only express the whims of its false freedom.

When you flow out into primordial consciousness, you are coupling it with wise innocence. With the total purity of BUDHI and infinite confidence. And just like that, your own life is your own message. YOGA BUDHI clearly shows that no mental ego can change the world, which itself is change and transience, but that each individual or image can transform itself. He who becomes aware of the reality of being, puts an end to fundamental ignorance, or the lack of self-identity. When connected through conscious consciousness, the dimension of conscious divinity opens, because we can recognize the body as what it IS, a vehicle in transience.

Primordial consciousness itself remains unchanged because it presents no expectation in the shadows. THERE IS NO REAL PAST. He who accepts the formless infinite conscious Now puts an end to memory and intellectual reason, assuming that his intelligence is active in non-mind and that the highest vibration of this intelligence is active; he suppresses and suspends all speculation, does not attach himself to the fruit of any action, and dies and is reborn in every instant moment. Neither the physical body nor the five sensory organs are essential to conscious consciousness.

Consciousness of the ONE GOD is pure. In the identified and conditioned individual, consciousness is individualized and the I is projected through the mind that sees two sides. Every mental process is limited by the duality not connected to the SUPREME TRUTH; thus, whereas individualized consciousness is only an APPEARANCE of primordial and infinite conscious consciousness, we find a definite correspondence between the laws and phenomena of the various states of the SOUL and LIFE.

On the physical level, everything vibrates; this is mind and movement. In this three-dimensionality of height, length and width perceived by the senses, conditioning and mental beliefs influence the person and project their inclinations.

Once we manage to ACCEPT that the psychological linear time of mental relationships all comes together in the present, we have taken a quantum leap; only in this way can we open up to fundamental reality, the consciousness of HERE NOW, or Instant Timelessness, which needs no support because it is empty.

At this P.O.I.N.T., what emerges is DHARMA, because it is bound to the moment itself, as always new, with no possibility of bitterness or resentment.

The Cause of Illusion

The whole is not dual, it is absolute and indivisible. Polarity is a figment of the mind that sees "Two Sides." All the opposites that may arise are imagined to be related and antagonistic; in other words, they are the same. Whenever you are at one extreme, sooner or later you will touch "the imaginary other extreme"; whenever you're fighting against SOMETHING you are like that something, which is nothing more than your own divided individual mind. It is the egoic mental personality that in the dense form is the protagonist of a duality; however, rhythm operates in the time conceived by the I, and cycles manifest to compensate based on CAUSATION, (each cause has its effect).

Everything in the realm of form is transitory and impermanent, which means THAT IT IS NOT REAL. Fundamental ignorance about oneself, about the world, and about the ONE GOD are inclinations of the mind, removed from the moment of consciousness itself. The ONE GOD is omnipresent in space without ceasing, without separation. Omniscient and omnipotent. Immutable. Not subject to change.

Whatever is conditioned is no longer totality. The only reality behind what we call CREATED, then, is the infinite primordial consciousness, a substrate of the whole. What is subject to conditioning is always the illusion of the separate part. What is created is doubtless mental, but has infinite primordial conscious consciousness as real substance; that is why it can be guaranteed that the essence is unity and that the two masculine and feminine aspects are simple phases of manifestation. There is no separation.

To grasp the cause of illusion, we can distinguish illusion as "SUPERIMPOSITION." This superimposition is no more than desire, because if there is no desire the moment itself is complete. Desire is superimposed through thought, or, identically seeks to bring into this moment that which is not currently manifesting itself.

This desire is what nullifies the enjoyment of what flows within you:

- ❖ It is outward-focused: transience.

- ❖ It is bound to the 5 senses.

- ❖ It seeks to remain in the past.

- ❖ It arises from the inclination of the mind seeing two sides to COMPARE.

- ❖ It lacks enjoyment.

- ❖ It relies on linear time.

- ❖ It makes the "I" feel threatened.

- ❖ It creates illusion to achieve goals and makes your joy as a person depend on those goals.

- ❖ It is a primary of the motor of the mind.

If you reject the idea of "I" and "THE WORLD," what transcends the duality of your own finite thought attached to the name and form, you will no longer be affected by objective desire.

To be affected by DESIRE you must pursue objects, and believe yourself to be THE DOER; such conditions generate the subject and the mental concern for the object of your desire, because you are imprisoned in the finite needs of the mind without realizing that you have in fact fabricated limitations upon yourself.

He who thinks he is a doer in any case is not; he thinks he does things and possesses things, but in fact he suffers because in this world nothing is permanent.

Desire is like a ghost that lures you toward the temporal future, excites the illusions of your ever non-present mind, gets you interested, and makes you see life as a cost. Until you perceive that the cause of your illusion is your own separate from the moment, your mind can't stop running, because the mental past continues to fuel it. The ability to transcend desire is the splendor of an end to illusion, or what you superimpose, in complete ignorance of the real consciousness of your being.

The teachings give the name of MAYA to the dreamer's dream. MAYA is identification with change. The fantasy of MAYA, which gives us the opportunity to dream, is in turn the feeling of separation. For the conditioned I, MAYA is the fascination that flux and transience exert on its individual mind, which sees "two sides." Starting from MAYA, the mental ego chooses a convenient direction and deviates from the natural course of things. The Ego is the separate part comparing itself; it therefore depends on external approval. And it feels threatened, because the mind-involved mind does not discern, but only rationalizes in proportion to its desire, and lets in separativity.

Leaving MAYA means pushing yourself towards spiritual realization and towards fundamentals. The uncorrected mind is directed toward attachment in transience, but the corrected mind is directed toward meditation.

When the impulse is towards spiritual realization, as the fundamentals, you open yourself to VICHARA, self-inquiry; the acceptance of the real renunciation, or the knowledge that you are not your body, and grasping that private desire is the cause of illusion - such is "The Way Out."

If this happens:

Meditate - Meditate - Meditate, as your relaxation. Until PRANA or (vital body) enters your heart and opens THE LOTUS OF LOVE which detains the thought. When divine love is manifest, what thought is needed? This love is limitless and unmoving. It is the selflessness and unconditionality that brings about the blossoming of your total understanding, forever, that you are FREE OF THREATS, it is a love that the word "love" fails to encompass. It is free of duality and poles, free of comings and goings; it is the TOTAL spectrum of energy and the infinite light of being.

This divine love is also sacred as the permanent presence of the one with no second; your only eternal security, your only true power. It is the one and only thing that has no opposite, because it is completely free of conceptualization, which can only occur within the limitations of time and space fabricated by the mind. And until you reach the last vestige of the mind, your "I" will not be free of Threats.

Consciousness itself is timeless, and it is what connects BUDHI with the eternal soul. Beyond time and limits, you are the divine presence. When BUDHI has become pure discernment, there is no illusion; then the cosmic intelligence in us is expressed. When you are fully receiving the impact of your own light, you can channel your desires and inclinations, and can thus avoid undertaking actions with any attachment to results.

Capture if BUDHI has matured in you, it will manifest the truth of consciousness, which expresses itself like an unaffected witness with no attachment to the body, because neither the body nor its desires are the ultimate goal of existence, even in waking life we are observer witnesses by nature. The omnipresent ONE GOD is the only doer, and since existence is in itself TOTAL, consciousness will always be the real factor.

A sanctified life is a life free of electivity because it is free of illusion.

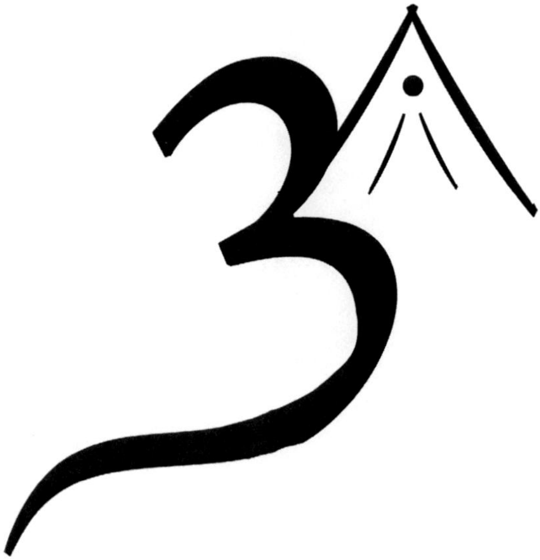

The Path of Vichara

VICHARA- the Path of Inquiry.

Toward the inward path, taking into account that mental, sensory, and bodily identification are only outward looking, to a transience with no reality to it because it is simply a projection of thought, which can be detained when PRANA or the vital body is introduced in the heart, and opens up the lotus of the heart.

Your whole transformation must take place -WITHIN- in order to transcend:

❖ The individual, or the image of consciousness

❖ The world or (object)

❖ Ignorance, or the veil or mass differentiation

And once it begins:

INQUIRE-INQUIRE-INQUIRE

And the individual mind will abandon its desires for deceptive sensory pleasures that only feed the ego. In this process, energy is the active principle. Mind, energy and matter are related and linked. We all must and can develop our internal energy field, but to achieve this, we must die to the past to experience neutrality.

One converts energy oneself; whether into kindred forces, or into imprisoning forces.

When you die to the past, the energy of the present bestows upon you the discovery of YOUR OWN LIFE, this discovery allows you not to be affected by your surroundings. It is your conditioned mental I that reacts based on impressions from what has already happened. As we know, the past does not exist, yet the conditioned I uses it as a reference. This burden known as the "past" constitutes a major expenditure of energy because the ONE GOD is omnipresent NOW.

When we discover our internal energy field we turn toward THE SUPREME, and the ego must dissolve because it disperses energy towards superficiality.

In terms of energy the ego is projected out from the individual, and MAYA is projected out from nature, based on the illusion of apparent diversity. The most difficult job in life is to remove the ego cover capping the intellect.

When the energy "moves" free of desire, it FLOWS.

FLOWING is the art of being passive-receptive, without sluggishness or attachment. FLOWING means floating, without adverse thought. With an acceptance of the inevitability of the moment "AS IT IS." He who FLOWS may appear useless, but simply has no mental enemies and no competition.

On this path of VICHARA you continue inquiring and inquiring until there appears within you a feeling of gratitude for your own breath, which has the INTERNAL sound of the SOHAM MANTRA.

In Vedic teaching HAMSA is the "heavenly swan," vehicle of BRAHMA and symbol of SOHAM. This swan of purity has a perfectly white plumage, symbolizing its ability to bring release from duality.

SOHAM is the constant sound of breath inhaled and exhaled, which leads us to merge with the "other." Repeating SOHAM, "I AM HIM," SOHAM, I am him, with each inhaled breath, "he" is attracted, and merges with me, and with each exhalation, "I" am impelled towards "Him," thus becoming us. In this way, we both become O.N.E. and duality is transcended.

SO and HAM merge into OM the basic vibration and symbol of BRAHMAN, the nameless and formless divinity: the indivisible all-pervading absolute, the base on which the universe rests. SHAKTI is its dynamism, with which it has no separation, just as MAYA and SHAKTI are also not separate.

In its deepest essence, the SOHAM mantra consists of two words:

SO: Equivalent to SAH, meaning "Him," as in BRAHMAN,

AND

HAM: Equivalent to A-HAM, meaning the "REAL SELF"

This deep meaning "IS" "I AM HIM" thus the consciousness grows within you and AHAMKARA (the ego) will cease to be a nuisance to you.

"I AM HIM," meaning the consciousness of the indivisible whole, demonstrates the sacred vision of HIRANYAGARBHA; when you go deeper and merge into HIRANYAGARABHA in conscious and loving union with EVERYTHING, learn its 14 spiritual laws and come to know BRAHMAN, you can only become BRAHMAN; then "THE POSTURE" of tolerance installs in the heart where the one god dwells as the being of all beings.

Thus, conscious breath is the presence of God within each of us, with no differentiation:

Inhaling - OM

and

Exhaling - OM

Thus internal consciousness arises.

Conscious breathing is what drops the mind into nothingness, steadily growing divine presence, the present and peace. When you merge, you perceive that EVERYTHING is OM, the sound that comes from silence and with OM consciousness there arises a spiritual conviction about our true nature: DIVINITY.

OM consciousness is the remedy to all suffering because it leads you to the fullness of whats real.

Thus you keep inquiring and inquiring until your gratitude is so immense that it encompasses experiences of pain as well, because both have the same transitory nature. Your mental ego, which had leaned more towards a preference for PLEASURE, had rejected pain; but that in fact only led to the rejected pain taking a leading role in your life without you realizing it.

As life appears to work in opposites because the mind sees two sides, if one seeks ONLY PLEASURE, it is in fact psychologically seeking "the pain" which never disappeared from the opposite end, so it becomes the most relevant.

If one can be grateful to both, they both disappear.

The satisfaction and gratification of desires prolongs fundamental ignorance because there is no end to the deception of the senses, and because the mind agitatedly maintains its objective IDEAS as anticipated goals.

The inquirer, that you are, dwells in PURE consciousness, unaffected by the predispositions of the body and what we call mind. From the consciousness of your atmic being, what does it matter whether the world APPEARS or not? As the world is a manifestation of being, it is irrelevant to the conscious inquirer whether or not being manifests itself in the world.

We know that thoughts obstruct the experience of pure consciousness, but VICHARA, or self-inquiry, can dissolve this obstruction. You INQUIRE so that pure consciousness and perceptual consciousness become one and the same. As the mind is the reflector, if it plunges back into its own source, thought disappears.

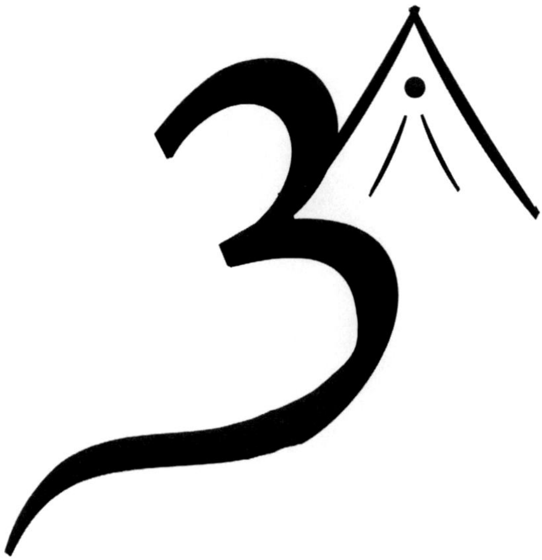

Judgement and Play

In YOGA BUDHI one perceives that JUDGMENT begins and ends in the mind that sees two sides through the individual personality experiencing feelings of separation. What becomes an uncertainty for the mental ego as (a separate part) or (fragment) is judged on the basis of a partial vision, although this conditioned "I" considers that to be necessary and adequate due to its condition. The ONE GOD is eternally realized without beginning or end; it never began and will never end. Its infinite light is substrate and witness. As an indivisible absolute, it never engages with what we call creation, yet never ceases to be its substrate.

He who is impelled towards spiritual realization through VICHARA and manages to - TAKE REFUGE - achieves the PLAY of existence without leaving any trace; forgetting everything else, and carrying no burdens.

Judgment is an inclination of a rational intellect that has not matured, the clouded jewel; but judgment should not be confused with the capacity for judgment. Judging is simply a mechanism of the conditioned world brought about by the dual nature of the split mind (the dual mind) bearing a psychological burden and absent from the present. An always-timeworn mind reflecting itself. Nor should we confuse the term JUDGMENT in this case with the procedures of HUMAN LAW. The conditioned human needs regulation by the LAW, to balance his impulsiveness, and one who TAKES REFUGE has no moral collision with this LAW.

The term PLAY, which in YOGA BUDHI refers to the nature of the spiritual heart absent from pretense, is very different.

If you can receive the light of your being you immediately perceive that it is a game, a divine leelas, a temporal joke.

If there is a closer look and inquire most profoundly, you can see that it is a game that has been played, and it is only because the mind looks at two sides that it continues to bear the burden of the past, translated as the path of the I, identified with the need for approval. The past is the logical consequence of the "I" that thinks it is a doer and possessor; this past is what sustains its desire. He who does not know that he already IS will fight to become something on the surface. In order to be able to abandon this judgment of reflections and enter into play, one must go through a process of healing one's mental wounds, and release the past by accepting what it is. But in play, the (form) disappears and the existential (the void) appears without leaving a trace. Judgment requires support, play has no support; as an analogy, we can look at the examples of DHARMA and KARMA. DHARMA is fluid emptiness, while the KARMA of the thinker within DHARMA is elective. An action conceived in the void with DEVOTION, only DHARMA is fluid; the leap from KARMA to DHARMA is always possible, because infinite and empty consciousness is what really "IS."

Identification with name and form begins and ends in the sensory mental ego because it has been subject to a deception. Thought is NOT REAL, and stopping thoughts through spiritual practice is the only thing that leaves us in pure VACUITY. As long as you are ruled by thought, projections of the selfish sentiment of "I" and "MINE" will always remain, with no US; and in this light, the "I" has only AN IDEA about what GOD IS.

This individual "I" or IMAGE, with its idea of what GOD IS, projects the movement of matter-focused thought, and can generate all kinds of theories according to what its still-immature intellect may decipher and understand, as determined by its environment. But this "I" is not aware of its own consciousness or infinite substrate. Its whole debate is a mere struggle of reflexes, following the facts to wherever its particular interest may bounce.

The individual or image that has not recognized its being is defensive; its mind deals with subjects and material concerns, and has goals and expectations it seeks to achieve in linear time. This individual, then, has never united passivity and receptivity within himself, and for this reason he has NOT BEEN ABLE TO PERCEIVE THE ILLUSION OF THE WORLD, and the mind is divided between its attractions and its repulsions. As long as this duality of attraction and repulsion remains within you, JUDGMENT remains possible. Beyond this duality there appears your uniqueness, and with it, SELF-CONFIDENCE which completes you, with no separation and with no need for comparison. That is where THE SEARCH comes to an end, because with self-confidence it is understood that ATMA, the real I, is at rest; it has no contamination caused by ego-thought projected by illusion.

It was the mental ego that was measuring both itself and the reflexes. So the ego was the experimenter, not the witness. When the objective illusion of the world fades, that means that the mind as a subject IS NO LONGER MISSING, because when there is no (subjective mind) there is also no (material object) seen as separate.

Only then can you be the infinite consciousness that you have always been, and there will be no way to distract you (seen as separate).

At this P.O.I.N.T.:

- ❖ There is no desire

- ❖ There is no possession

- ❖ There is no deceiving

- ❖ There is no fear

- ❖ No feeling of loss or of failure manifests; one SIMPLY IS, in the timeless Now, as the fundamental reality where thought DOES NOT EXIST as an obstruction. This apparent succession of moments is in fact Eternal Now; the freedom of self-confidence is an internal exercise of indivisible and radiant being in ANANDA, not some superficial and ideological concept backed by a kind of system also blinded by itself. Freedom is like a ladder to climb only for the rational intellect without self-knowledge; in fact freedom resides in absolute indivisible oneness. The notion of individuality that corresponds to the separate part is then lost; a being that has become Aware is ALERT and all encompassing. All differentiation for being or ATMA is mere appearance; there is thus nothing to JUDGE in such appearance. In Being, there is no sense of differences. The realization of BEING is found in BEING, and not in SEEING BEING.

If for one moment you can grasp that freedom, you have grasped the infinite. Then, all images will disappear, and with them your fear, because it was hidden in your imagined slavery.

YOU HAVE ALREADY GIVEN UP. YOU HAVE ALREADY SURRENDERED. NOW ALL THERE IS TO DO IS PLAY, AND PLAY CONSCIOUSLY.

Conditioning

In YOGA BUDHI you have discovered that impetus is the driving force of the stage play of evolution conscious consciousness, is a tendency. You have recognized that life is the ONE GOD PLAYING, and the past is opression, because it is always the (retrospective-retroactive or timeworn mind). Finding support in unresolved painful experiences that have failed to for the conditioned I, as its own conditioning pattern in the PLAY; the new mind of each moment is analogous to a spotless mirror, because it does not categorize or compare the reflection, but simply FLOWS, ALERT. If you accept your mind as simply a useful tool for the moment itself, what we call the APPARENT WORLD is but the mind itself and its inclinations, rooted in the timeworn mind or dusty mirror.

This mind impresses into memory everything it looks at, and builds a structural conceptualization with little flexibility. When all your behavior in the game of life is based on rigidity, your whole life is based on conditioning.

CONDITIONING means putting personal conditions on the moment due to the psychological burden of the past (the timeworn mind, or the dust on the mirror), or your personal fabrications placed upon the spontaneity of the heart. Due to conditioning, your thoughts - your words - and your deeds are misaligned; often you may know something in your heart, but end up doing the opposite because of your conditioning. The conditioning generates your struggle, your emotional conflicts and your insecurity, and it is precisely because of that insecurity that things that happen in the periphery can hurt you.

Developing a sense of self-security means opening your eyes to see that your conditioning IMPRISONS YOU. Developing self-security is a matter of rescuing what is authentic in you (the totality), integrated consciousness, which never changes.

Your struggle is conditioned by what you THINK IT IS.

Your emotional conflicts are conditioned by your mixed feelings.

If you've thrown out everything from your mind except what is happening right now, this means it is not conditioned by appearances. A natural mind IS CONSCIOUSNESS.

Due to conditioned action, the manifested universe is mental, with a broad pattern of determinism, but within a SPACE-TIME-CAUSATION MATRIX. In this world everything you see is cause and effect. All stories occur in this matrix; nothing happens by chance. In a given space and in a given time, you won't encounter anyone again by chance.

IN YOGA-BUDHI the cultivating tools can be found:

- ❖ Meditate as daily relaxation

  and

- ❖ Inquire as evolution towards consciousness.

You can meditate and inquire until your daily activity becomes a MEDITATIVE LIFE.

You have already seen that the apparent world causes frustration by identification, by generating need.

You have already seen that everyone who seeks satisfaction in the apparent and conditioned world "FAILS," because they do so through the ego or idea of the thinking I. This conditioned world is based on a structure that is also relative, or entirely molded by fixed patterns previously antagonistic to one another.

You have already seen that contradictions are inevitable; such is the nature of the world and of the mind, but they become apparent, and only when by releasing the ego, you free yourself from duality:

(PLEASURE - PAIN)

You have already seen that the I experiences a feeling of separation because you dream of an apparent world supported by a supposed independent reality, or relativism. The old mind reacts to transient things based on its conditioning. In the actual center of the light the thinker cancels itself out, and you can persevere, without being constantly assailed by apparent contradictions.

To make your daily life a MEDITATIVE LIFE, you've had to recognize that a DESIRING MIND IS NON-MEDITATIVE, because in such case, consciousness becomes aware of itself at the same moment as it forgets itself as an object of perception.

Those who embark on a MEDITATIVE LIFE must understand the universality of their being, which is beyond hope and despair, doubt and uncertainty. They do not waste time drawing conclusions because they simply flow in all directions and in none. So, all conclusions enslave. The individual was only an image seeking to satisfy its needs in the world through the MIRROR that is the mind. Its failure was that it was looking outward for reality, because it adhered to external forms, which are transitory.

As long as there is illusion there will be disillusionment, and as long as there is conditioning there will be pain, because everything relative is subject to change. As your spiritual direction is oriented towards the ONE GOD, neither your intellectual abilities nor any accumulation of money can define your intimate relationship to that ONENESS. One cannot speak of meditating without having experience with meditation oneself.

TO MEDITATE - is to be above desires without the slightest trace of superiority.

TO MEDITATE - is to remain in the invariable center, WITH NO TIME PENDING OR SPACE DEPENDING.

If you have taken refuge in BUDHI you have inquired, you have meditated, you have gone through illusion and merged into the whole.

There is no longer "SUBJECT" and "OBJECT" as separate; there is only existence without the limits of name and form. Here, the doings of the mind have disappeared and there is only the being of consciousness. Emptiness without support has now become possible, and when emptiness without support appears, all conditioning has disappeared, right now. The moment has become eternity, without limit and without momentum. It is a definitive metamorphosis.

If you wish to understand what conditioning is, in essence, it is the force that imprisons. Anyone with ATTACHMENT to sensory perception, has been CONDITIONING the false sensation of their conditioned reason. It is only your ego that hungers for the limelight and for recognition in the conditioned environment.

Mindless Attention

One, with no counterpart. The supreme being is absolute and relative at the same time; consciousness is the substrate of the whole.

If your attention is directed towards the absolute, you have merged, but if your attention is directed towards the relative, it is because the mind conceals the real nature of being, creating an illusory appearance. It is impossible to grasp the meaning of truth that way.

The mind is a knot of individual desires, its strategem is to project ENDLESS UNCERTAINTY. Your task is to avoid getting caught in its webs.

When you observe it from a distance you perceive its duality (it either elevates or sinks you), because it is full of appetites and claims. If you learn to see everything as insignificant you discover that in your real center there is only equanimity.

When BUDHI shows itself as rational, the "I" due to its condition believes itself to hold the truth, and even comes to think that this partial truth can antagonize other truths; but "The Truth" is not the same thing as your truth, concocted by an impure intellect.

The mind must be purified of its ambition and its past; only then can wisdom emerge in the present. Thus the only supreme goal is to REALIZE BEING.

The limits of the mind are always superimposed on your unlimited potential. Mindless mind depends on nothing, and when your innocence emerges you no longer have anything to prove; all your mindless attention merges into the moment of consciousness, with no separation.

To be yourself is to remain in the equanimous center, such is the art of non-electivity. Constant satisfaction, absence of goals, non-intention. Because all forms are "ONE," you will find bliss by merging with the supreme will, rooted in the impermanence of mind that dwells nowhere yet excludes nothing, a witness to the whole.

You thus have nothing to prove to someone who does not know himself, and have much love and unlimited tolerance to share.

When you are nothing in mind, you are everything in conscious consciousness; with that understanding of totality comes the manifestation of SPIRITUAL BEAUTY, as a virtue of your wise equanimity united to all things beyond names and forms.

That absolute attention to the moment of consciousness until you become lost IS TOTALITY. And in that totality you can respect virtues and defects without losing spiritual character. You are no longer there, and when you are not there, the totality is there. Only the intention of the ego "stuck in the middle" kept you from seeing it, because its feeling of the doer IS SEPARATE FROM THE MOMENT.

KEEP THIS PRESENT:

No one awake to consciousness says

"I" and "MY" about the ever-changing world, because consciousness is total and possession is partial. You are total when you are aware that YOU ARE NOT THE DOER AND YOU ARE NOT THE POSSESSOR. You only respond to what happens NOW. Your totality is no longer mental. It is not dual. It does not speculate. The conditioned I limits the ONE GOD with its assumptions. Your reality is not limited.

The entertainments of the intellectual mind and the projections of its abilities are what we call "mundane life"; while you are identified with the world, the world continues to attract you. It is up to each person to either live a mundane life with identification or a spiritual life with an identity of their own.

The totality is divine presence in its continuous flow, free of any fragmentation. Without totality the ego experiences the feeling of separation, where it believes that it "does" and "possesses" with attachment. It is this ego that suffers when it does not get what it wants in its limited mental scope. This shows that it is not the doer.

When your attention goes to the world, the ego engages with thought, and only thought, as if it were essential, and in turn just projects the thought that there is (a beginning and an end). Beyond thought, nothing begins or ends. In fact:

YOU CANNOT CONCEIVE OF INFINITY.

Such is the guarantee that existence is always simply existence. With no limitations of name and form.

Be aware of it

Only being limited by the thought that it is the most important thing from the perspective of your intellectual reason makes you perceive "this" world as if it were a reality. And hence you entertain yourself by looking "outward" as if it were something real.

This need for control and appearances in a world limited by thought is called SELF-IMPORTANCE because the truth is that the individual person controls nothing; his intellect is deceived by his own thinking.

All the reactionaries that emerge in the world are influenced by this deception. They are sick with self-importance, which implies either that they do not believe in god, or that they see god as something utilitarian. Self-importance makes them believe that they control what is in fact out of their hands, since there is a space - time - causation matrix, and one single omnipresent god, never a broad pattern of determinism outside that matrix.

With the mind, the whole struggle of the conditioned I is based on the fact that it wants to become something that has come "from outside" because it ignores that it is already (inside) and in the infinite there is no limit. The phenomenon of wanting to become something iconic is accompanied by repression, because the I seeks to satisfy certain expectations that do not belong to "it."

Not accepting who you ARE, you become dependent on the external circumstances that drag you along psychologically, without ever discovering your own uniqueness.

Uniqueness means that you are unique in this existential game; even on the physical level each fingerprint is unique. We all have the opportunity to be authentic in our uniqueness without the need to envy anyone's projection. Quite the contrary, we can admire it.

Envy is born in comparison and in the feeling of inferiority, but only from the perspective of the totality can you see that each possibility is valid in itself. You always want to become something that has been shown to you, and very rarely does someone who has an authenticity all their own appear. This energy that you use on wanting to become SOMETHING is the same that you can use to develop your own creativity without needing to try to meet everyone's expectations.

YOUR ACCEPTANCE removes the conditions and puts an end to the struggle that causes your lack of attention to your own potential, which comes from divinity. If you incorporate actual renunciation, understanding and accepting in a mature manner that you are not your body, then all the psychological accumulation you have taken on by wanting to please everyone on the basis of your mind, body, and sensory senses will come to an end.

A broader dimension has emerged in you, and when there is no longer a clash between what you expect in your mind and what actually is, you have accepted who you are, because there is no longer conflict; your serenity has arisen in the face of the apparent world that is occurring.

Notice that without acceptance there are only burdens, because the antagonism begins within you, with whatever is happening.

Only when you accept who you are will you stop repressing yourself and seeking to become something else. In this acceptance, mental duality loses all its power of fascination, because it is an imagination of opposite extremes that extends only to the body, not to who you really are. Your character is the strength of the spirit of unity in everyday life, just as your genuine value is in the strength of divine beauty you have as a character trait.

The True "Gift" of the Renunciant

Though actual resignation consisted of realizing that you are not your body, the true "GIFT" of the renunciant is:

INDIFFERENCE TO THE CAPRICES OF THE MIND, which goes from one extreme to the other generating doubt and uncertainty.

You can become an observer of your own drama in your head without identifying yourself, without judging, and without trying to end it.

This "GIFT" is so powerful and full of potential because it teaches you to OBSERVE without worrying and without the need to get involved.

In this sense, all slavery is no more than the idea of an object and desire.

DESIRE + DISSATISFACTION = FRUSTRATION

With this "GIFT" in place, YOU WILL NEVER BE FRUSTRATED. The renunciant has understood that only if he awakens his consciousness can there be a real transformation, not merely a virtual change. In the real transformation you recognize that the fundamental reality is HERE/NOW; such is the ultimate existential gift. The gateway to immortal infinity.

HERE/NOW as consciousness and substrate is absent from conceptualization. It is unlimited stillness; and until you perceive that consciousness is the substrate of TIMELESS totality, the conditioned "I" will be bound to linear mental periods in time and space, coupled with logic.

First you will perceive that "past, today and future" are not about time, but rather are about the relationship of the mind as "MOVEMENT" and "DURATION":

PAST: This is nothing without memory. Memory is nothing without recollection. Your conditioned I all too often clings to the past and is thus altered. Generating a mood by recollection is also a superimposition or illusion. This past is non-existent, and as long as it pursues you, the mind will just have more fuel to burn.

TODAY: Occurs as the supposed basis of the mental ego that anticipates and goes up against contention and impatience. It is almost imperceptible, because your basis is still the past, as the anchor for the logical sequence in your image.

FUTURE: This is an uncertainty based on that logical sequence, which does not exist either. So, with no conscious connection, man is the architect of his apparent life through thought.

First, one ACCEPTS that this dual relationship (PAST - FUTURE) can only be projected by a mind with no NOW. In any of these three states "OBJECTS" exist in the presence of the dual mind and the deceptive senses. The BEING THAT IS YOU remains timeless and unaffected in the presence of objective transience.

If the mind is transcended as subject and concern of these linear objective occurrences, THOSE THREE PERIODS DISAPPEAR, and duration, known as time, no longer exists.

Memory-thought-intellect project THE STAGE that itself creates THE DRAMA. When you are coerced by memory, a thought emerges, which in turn generates an emotion and a mood, which are then analyzed through your prism of seeing things, or your rational intellect. What you don't realize is that all this IS DISTORTED.

Your mind needs duality and fabricates whatever it takes to achieve it. Your mind has been deceived by your senses. It sees the "OTHER" as separate because it seeks hierarchies. Beyond the mind and its essential duality, there is no separate other, but from within the mind, every person you see is a mirror reflecting you. This "OTHER," seen as separate, is the essential raw material for the projection of "DRAMA" upon the subject.

The OTHER that has not known actual renunciation needs to have the "OTHER" and see it as separate in order to release its frustration. Remember that.

Between one perceiving mind and another perceiving mind THERE IS ONLY FALSEHOOD. One idea versus another idea, one criterion against another criterion such is relativism.

But remember that it is only the divided mind in a world of appearances that projects guilt based on its own canons of relativity and morality, because such is the inclination of the mind that sees opposites.

When we TAKE REFUGE in BUDHI, "THE JEWEL," i.e., the individual, comes to DISCERN BALANCE AS PURITY OF MIND because it has developed the true gift of the renunciant. It has opened the channel to receive the light of ATMA and has thus become indifferent to the caprices of the mind. There is no longer any need to struggle with the intellect.

As long as YOU HAVE NOT TAKEN REFUGE, the other seen as separate IS YOUR MIRROR, because the mind reflects and is reflected. Only conscious consciousness reflects without being reflected.

This "mental reflection" projects itself as a PLOT in its identification with the "THREE STATES," reduced to "TWO" (past - future) by directional electivity.

The ego chooses the direction that is convenient for it, and ITS GREATEST CHALLENGE is to transcend this mental decision or directional electivity, because that electivity is what prevents it from opening itself to existence in all directions and none. In the world of directional selectivity and appearances, all kinds of things are happening; but this is only a product of the projection of thought and of ATTACHMENT.

If you open yourself to existence, your "I-IDEA" is removed from its context, and all expectations, premeditations, demands, superimposed objective needs, and even rejections cease to exist.

When you understand that everything is a combination of everything else, just as the same water from nature quenches the thirst of both the poor and the rich, there no longer remains anything to resolve in an unknown and temporal future, because without the relationships established by the mind, nothing is pending in TIME, and nothing is dependent upon SPACE. You are BEING-HERE-NOW. In this here-now, you have burned the veils, you have broken through the boundaries of NON-EXISTENCE. The now has no end; it never began - you were sleeping, unaware of existence, but existence was perfectly aware of you in YOUR SPIRITUAL HEART, WITH NO PRETENSION.

When that true gift of the renunciant manifests its purest expression, we abide full of blessings, for bliss needs no external stimulus to be blissful.

He who accepts a given event as it is, does not burden himself with the fact that it is already in the past.

In such acceptance, free of affectation, there is meditation.

Meditation is conscious consciousness free of burdens, the light of the spontaneous instant. In the internal posture, the focus of consciousness is fixed upon a single objective: BEING. In meditation you don't have one idea inside and another outside. When meditation emerges in the course of a seeker's inquiry, cosmic harmony begins to appear.

In meditation there is pure consciousness without content. Its complement is THE JOY OF SILENCE, where the noise of the ups and downs of the mind disappears. He who meditates has unveiled his center and can watch "THE MIND" go by without identifying himself with "THAT." The meditator knows that he is not the mind and its *vitris* (inclinations, or mental movements) because he focuses on the real self.

Your "I," conditioned and identified with names and forms, cannot (be the meditator) because it is continually burdened with two illusions:

❖ The illusion of being a doer in the material world,

AND

❖ The illusion of being a possessor in the material world.

The material world does not even exist as such; it is only the senses simulating the material state. The clouded jewel falls prey to the notion of "I AND MINE" with no "us." Such is selfishness. And it is always selfishness that seeks to control what one believes one does and possesses from the perspective of the sentiment of separation, in the world of material appearances, which is changing and transitory.

IN MEDITATION, THE DIVISION DISAPPEARS, and there is only connection. Love, compassion and tolerance are present together with humility. You merge into the being that is the being of all beings.

Understand that only meditation can restore you to THE PRESENT and its divine presence. With intense devotion to the supreme being, the ONE GOD with no counterpart, you are realizing the SUPREME form of meditation because you unite (body-mind-soul) with no particular mental goal. The fruit of meditation is called (SAHAJA VASTHA). This means that all actions originate from the consciousness of the one god, and not from the mind of the conditioned I.

Every meditator has before him a DAILY DISCIPLINE that consists in being ALERT AND VIGILANT TO HIS OR HER OWN INTERNAL DRAMA. This does not mean that you will become paralyzed, it means that you are already aware that you are not the doer, although the mind and the senses fool you into thinking the opposite. Full of joy and relaxation, each and every act becomes an offering of love to the ONE GOD.

When there is no mental goal, there is only celebration of the ever harmonious moment, with no separation, because in the essential game, there are no two separate wills. There is only the DIVINE will, which is not realizing elective KARMA, and has no attachment to results of any kind.

Meditation is DHYANA - uninterrupted alertness in conscious consciousness, an interaction of knowledge, an exact tuning to the wavelength of the divine, filling you with bliss.

That conscious alertness of BEING has no need for EXTERNAL ATTENTION; it is the non-material "center posture." That center only appears when you withdraw yourself from your mind and its imagined opposites.

In DHYANA and its meditative alertness "THREE" merge into one:

❖ The object of meditation.

❖ The process of meditating.

❖ The meditator himself.

In DHYANA, all feelings of difference and separation are annulled despite the enormous apparent diversity.

When there is INWARD concentration you discover (YOUR OWN LIFE); but if there is outward dispersion, the (lives of others) drag you down due to emotionality and sentimentality. Your meditation can only FIND REST in the spiritual heart, AND IF THERE IS REST, it is because THERE IS NO EGO.

With that rest of the heart you have harmonized with the whole without wanting to become anything; thus you have discovered an inexpressible silence - YOGA as the understanding of YOGA BUDHI unity.

This leads you to the center of the real self. When the mind and its dominion over you cease, it leads you to merge with the whole. It leads you to transcendence of the partial, to your real inner order, to your surrender to the omnipresent, to true freedom without dualities. To an end to the mind's agitation, at last forgotten. To the divinity that you are.

"The ups and downs" are detained. They have all been integrated into a united oneness, and when you have reached true love in your heart, thought HAS DETAINED.

HERE/NOW - solitude is the presence of oneself as god, IN EVERYTHING. When you reach the center of your being, unconditional and unegotistical love emerge, the supreme bliss of non-reliance on any external stimulus, with no separation, infinite goodness and the joy of blessed silence. Every moment is an external celebration of BEING, because there is no sense of differences. Being dwells in everything.

The Limitation of Thought

From the perspective of the mind, you cannot perceive that thought itself is the limit, because thinking is all the mind can do. The world projected from thought is NOT real. YOU, here TODAY, can never conceive of infinity. Only existence without limits is free. It would thus be quite difficult for you to ACCEPT that the ONE GOD is experience absent from thought, because your entire duration is based on continuous bombardment by thoughts in your head.

It is thought that has a beginning and an end. If you grasp and discern, from your permanent core, that your thoughts can be observed like passing clouds drifting through the infinite sky, you can see that thought is not real either.

It will always be a shock to the ego to accept that the thinker is not important, because if you stop following your thoughts, then (the world that they project) where they are discussed, claimed, opined and argued over, will no longer exist for you. Only in the world of limits do all those things seem necessary.

The mind must either fight or flee, if you neither fight nor flee, you simply remain without thoughts, and there is conscious alertness as an observer witness. The thinker is always limited by a "beginning and end," because the one unique reality has no duration and is not dual. In the world of the thinker, duration is everything, but in reality there is only permanent stillness; that is why the guarantee of existence is that it cannot be interrupted.

"What moves is the mind," and from the perspective of that "stillness" no movement is real or significant; everything will change, everything will transit, everything will pass.

When you discover your oneness, you immediately stop comparing yourself iconically, because you also discover oneness in everything, the great divine game, the great joke of temporality.

Being is always being, and dwells in everything without having to become anything and without having to reach any transitional objective. When you know that you are unique, matter DOES NOT DEFINE YOU. Matter, after all, is no more than the density of the mind through the combination of the five elements: ETHER, AIR, FIRE, WATER, EARTH. Although you will become enlightened at the instant you become aware of your oneness, you will continue to flow with the harmony of the universal mind with no conflict. There is no conflict when you know that your oneness is fused with this very moment of conscious consciousness; even though millions of IDEAS and thoughts may sprout up, because you are now the meditator you know that you can simply observe from your core. When we say that what moves is the mind, what is moving, we know, is that dual temperament. We are referring to the movement of mental illusion into a mental future of one who thinks he is the doer of a mental past.

The conditioned I believes that this past is referential, or that it is indicated by what it has now become in the apparent world, (a deception); in fact what you call TIME is merely a human psychological expression that prepares the way for the occurrence of thought through the thinker. It is always thought that builds within you an elective directional impulse in favor of the ego, preventing you from seeing that the possibilities are endless. Here, your logic becomes your prison. Beyond this impulse, trust in existence is unwavering.

Your thinking cannot simply play as it comes free of antagonism with time and space. Thus the ego and the individual mind of the image are the limit of play, which can be translated as a denial of fluidity, because the thinker has never seen the center.

The ego does not exist. The limit does not exist. But although you may not find your real center, you get the impression that there is existence through the ego.

You may either think you are alive from the perspective of the mind, or you may know that you exist from the perspective of consciousness. Identification is the antithesis of identity.

The mind is a speculative system that seeks to manipulate; conscious consciousness is disinterested fluidity.

Ego and mind project the dynamics of interest and compromise. And whenever there is interest, there is servility and fantasy.

In HERE/NOW, the fundamental reality, SPACE and TIME disappear, because there is no temporary movement of any thinker or fictitious possessor. When we say that the mind must be purified, we are observing that conditioned ambition plunges the "I" into psychological mental time as a relationship of the divided mind of the moment of conscious consciousness itself. As the ambition of this "I" is conditional, it must think about what it calls the FUTURE.

We already know that only meditation can return you to THE PRESENT, so this apparent world, projected from relativism, the illusion of the doer and the illusion of the possessor, IS SUPERFICIAL, and NEVER touches the internal reality.

If you have come to know the INTERNAL reality, you exist in the uninterrupted conscious consciousness of SAT-CHIT-ANANDA, as eternal contemplation free of duality and separation. If you still have not come to know your inner reality, the mind manifests only concern for transitory objects, and the mind simply has a need to be controlled, as it goes on showing off and being hypocritical.

> The only danger you face, that is that you may fall victim to your own mind. Such victimization is always simply god self-limiting by judging and punishing.

I assure you that if you assume control of your mind as a useful tool at the moment of conscious consciousness, it becomes an instrument of transcendence.

From the center, BEING is infinite; from duality the EGO mind is FINITE (your deception of the beginning and end)

> In that center, there is nothing to know apart from your-self. There is nothing to achieve separate from yourself. Here/now is the only thing that does not transit, the only thing that neither comes from anywhere, nor goes anywhere.

> But if the mind of he who thinks he is a doer goes into movement or creates expectations, the now is forgotten, and desire and illusion arise within you.

ETERNAL WITNESS exceeds the mind; he who exists in the NOW does not think of the NOW. He who transcends the directional electivity of the convenient ego teaches without words and "works without action" and without "private goals." Only DHARMIC love and righteousness are eternal. Peace comes through VIVEKA (discernment) and VAYRAYA (detachment).

From SHANTI - peace - you pass to PRASHANTI: the abode of eternal peace; from PRASHANTI, you pass to PRAKANTI: the effulgence; from PRAKANTI, you pass to PARAMJOTI: the divine light. That light of oneness with no counterpart is a permanent presence in the dimension of being, which can be called CAUSELESS JOY beyond any imaginable duality.

Thousands of paths may appear, but there is only one master key: THE ACCEPTANCE THAT GIVES WAY TO SURRENDER, TO SARANAGATI, GIVING YOURSELF UP ENTIRELY; when you surrender, you are not there - the only thing that exists is the TOTALITY.

He who accepts the moment - the only "goal of life" - will know no calamity outside the moment.

This thinking of the "I" that arises in the heart is an APPEARANCE of being. One thought changes another, be it positive or negative.

If thought dissolves, the thinker disappears and there remains only the love that has always existed in undiluted, primordial, essential being. All unhappiness was a natural effect arising as a consequence of mental duality and nothing else. Where there is no longer the one and the conditioned "I," there is ONLY the contemplative NOW.

Where there is a conditioned "I," the ego concentrates on the mental wounds burdening it, because it believes they have harmed it.

If you come to rest, in the being of the thinker there will be no thought. Thought is only a cloud, which cannot destroy the sky. Thought, together with feeling, is incessantly changing within you. Everything in the world projected by thought is change; if you manage to discern what it is that changes, THE WITNESS is the discerner, at that point movement comes to an end for you. It is thought itself that must stop; you must become aware of your own thinking process, without struggle and without repression.

THE PRESENT IS YOUR PRESENCE

Before what you conceive as creation, there existed only primordial consciousness without form. The idea of creation is born when pure knowledge decides to play at manifestation.

That PURE knowledge never ceases to be what it is. The object is the intent behind the pronunciation of the word, and the form goes on as consciousness, giving meaning to the word in time-and-space.

If in an instant you perceive that before what is called creation there is only silence, THE PRESENT means the absence of pretension, because all your attention is here in this same omnipresent moment.

That is why only MEDITATION can return you to it. Only in the absence of pretense can you develop a vigilant consciousness of this moment, free of ideas, cultivating a meditative life in harmony with omnipresence. When your mind has been purified, nothing is pending a linear mental future. Everything that your mind wants to achieve on the relative surface separates you from the present and its presence.

If all your mental ambition dissolves, what emerges is the permanence of this moment itself, without any premeditation.

If you already know that what reflects without being reflected is consciousness, wherever your individual image is reflected YOUR MYSTERY APPEARS, or (that which shows your unresolved part). The consciousness that permeates everything simultaneously, does not claim to be rewarded, expects nothing from anyone, and is not reflected in any attitude, nor threatened by any condition. Consciousness knows itself.

For example, humility is conscious because it does not intend to change anything. So the duality of the mind is the fantasy in this whole equation. If oneness of character arises in you, it is because you have seen the present, and have understood "the world" as pure consciousness, which means that it has ceased to be seen as an object perceived as separate; consequently there is also no subject (mind). This puts an end to the most deceitful duality. And with the end of the most deceitful duality, SPIRITUAL MATURITY appears, free of spiritualism. It is totality without limit, absolute bliss WITHOUT MAYA.

NOW

YOU ARE AN INFINITE CENTER WITHOUT FORM.

You are absolute nectar to share and celebrate that "we are all one" with sincerity.

Your own being is bliss. Your oneness of character is spiritual function with all things.

Since MAYA is the mind's fascination with temporality, the perception of MAYA can bear witness only to timeworn things.

The ego was trapped in this objective illusion, and for that reason it believed that it was making progress on the surface, by accumulating and controlling objects. The illusion was in the feeling of separation and in identification with what is in constant flux.

By taking REFUGE IN BUDHI, your internal guide is activated, and the external events that pass as appearances will no longer affect you as significant obstacles on the road to understanding oneness. The following are and have always been the obstacles:

- ❖ Selfishness, which separates you from love

  AND

- ❖ Possessiveness, which draws you toward ambition and greed.

In this selfishness and possessiveness the mind sees itself as excluded and becomes exclusive, as a "separate part," stimulating fragmentation more and more. The ego cannot conceive "good without evil," and is always divided between one thing and another; it is this psychological division that generates doubtful uncertainty as the limit of intellect and reason.

Only in your present can you accept the harmony of your heart where the constant celebration of being is independent of the external world, because there is no need for attachment to the fruits of any action.

> In your presence in the present, your highest meditation has fused your devotion with indivisible absolute being. This is pure consciousness without content, pure emptiness without support.

All spirituality is synthesized in the understanding grasped and discerned in the center or permanent reality. Formless god. Non-mind. Light as substrate and witness. The absence of desire. The immutable source. The unchanging permanence of pure love. They are all the same. When you discover your centered stillness you have also discovered that all that is manifested that distances itself from love does so only out of ignorance and selfishness. What is authentic, because it is authentic, opposes nothing.

Faith and trust accompany that authenticity, which is not contaminated because everything is infinite consciousness.

Only with faith and trust will you understand that the ONE GOD is received in your heart as love without confusion.

That love is always linked to your DHARMIC righteousness, because it begins with you and you have shared with everything.

Having faith is not the same as believing; belief establishes itself based on a duality (subject-object), and the believer can change beliefs.

Faith coupled with trust is the antidote to fear. Faith is from the heart. Belief is from the head. If your reason is confined, you are on the absent edge of the center.

You thus come to believe that everything is about the logical end of your personal point of view, and deceive yourself.

A confined believer is oriented towards thought. You thus develop a need to approve and be approved, and may become attached to the illusion of considering everything that does not match your point of view to be inferior. All ideological or religious fundamentalism is linked to belief, confined within REASON.

Anger, hate, envy, selfishness, greed, cunning, resentment, jealousy, rancor; all these are emotions found in the individual as IMAGE, but these emotions can be burned away by intense devotion.

The key here is to purify the mind to make that leap, because your individual conditioned "I" without an identity of its own is like a wave of (mind-emotion) seeking to control the uncontrollable.

When you align thought, word and deed, you begin to activate the present that you yourself have refused psychologically without realizing it. As the world is a forest of words, he who sees differences in caste, color, creed, race and religion is locked within his own reason. As long as your intellect is locked up, it cannot discern beyond differences, because it will be fueled by concepts, arguments, thoughts, and words.

It is always your two-sided mind that creates expectations and demands about this forest of words called the world, and it is always conditioning that prevents you from harmonizing with peace.

Only through the absence of pretense and meditation can you return.

Have you never noticed that your fear comes from your own intention? The mind in its intention has a dogma, it always believes that it has to be completed, and what is incomplete fabricates fear from the perspective of the separate part. Fear refers to intention and meaning because it includes a threat based on a polarized ambiguity. What is beyond polarities, its imagined meaning and intention, does not engender fear. If you learn to alternate between opposites they never touch you; they belong to appearances. They can never simply stay bound to one place.

> THE ONLY THING THAT CAN STAY YOUNG FOREVER IS "PLAY" WHICH IN YOGA BUDHI REFERS TO HARMONY WITH THE SPIRITUAL HEART, FREE OF PRETENSION.

In this PLAY, form disappears, and emptiness without support appears; it is always lively, is always enthusiastic in disposition, with no need for psychological motivation, and always nourishes itself in moderation. Without play, you have lost the opportunity to stay young forever.

Total attention to the moment until you lose yourself is your most powerful tool; play and play, knowing that you are neither your mind nor your body, and will end up in BEING. A false man, not recognizing his being, can only fabricate a false structure. This is the meaning of APPEARANCE, where the present and its presence are not known.

The Great Key Code

There is one great key:

NEVER STRUGGLE,

JUST BECOME CONSCIOUSNESS.

Whenever you are struggling against something, you are reflecting without accepting. ACCEPTANCE is the feeling of feelings. It means removing your condition, not imposing your desire, because by attempting to impose it, your DISTURBANCE and RESTLESSNESS arise. Conditioning, attachments, and the coercion of labels are always in the middle of your acceptance. Acceptance is rewarding because it harmonizes with your consciousness evolution. This will prepare the way for the transformation that guides you toward BEING. Only with acceptance will you learn to FLOW with the natural course of things.

When you struggle without acceptance, it is as if you are at one end and the object of your struggle is at the other; you have not noticed that what you gravitate toward is unimportant to others.

And that is the important detail: struggle is egoic and directional; it implies fear due to intention, and has meaning only from separateness.

The supreme lesson to be learned in this world is how to understand and transcend mental duality, to find the missing link to that consciousness that knows itself to underlie all things and has no need to engage.

And such is the supreme lesson, because in discerning it, it emerges that all the opposite extremes ARE IMAGINARY. It is only the divided mind that sees two sides that makes it seem to you that "life" is good and "death" is bad. The cause of these imaginings is that the mind accumulates impressions and desires that it seeks to obtain in life through the physical body; the human personality also does not want to part with what it believes to be its own. As almost no one knows when their death will come, the mind creates the struggle to not die, and continues along submerged in duality. In the apparent world, everything seems to be about opposites, but if for a moment you accept both sides at the same time you will realize that you cannot really divide existence, because what is guaranteed in existence is that it cannot be fathomed in thought. It always transcends duality without leaving a trace.

As soon as it seeks to fathom existence, the mind's understanding is weak and incomplete. You must go beyond the duality of the mind to comprehend that everything is infinite consciousness without division. What stands between you and all of existence is precisely mental duality; an illusion. You can embark on a practice of daily POSITIVITY, including:

- ❖ Keeping suitable and harmonic company

- ❖ Moderate consumption of nutritious foods

- ❖ Sensible regulation of behavior in relation to your surroundings

- ❖ Developing the observer witness to your own internal drama

With a daily practice of positivity, constant gratitude emerges and the duality of the mind disintegrates, because little by little an energetic neutrality emerges, and with it an acceptance of the totality with no pretension.

> The oneness of existence guarantees that a realized vision is a vision of unity, and direct harmonization requires no intervention by thought. You can trust in existence, because it flows with no particular desire, here/now. Oneness is absolute and indivisible, and has no counterpart.

On this path of BUDHI Yoga you can come to understand that it is your mind that seeks to reflect everything, because it sees a mirror in each personality. The mind tries to reflect everything except you as reality, because if you become aware of yourself, there can be no mental reflection. The image and the mirror disappear, you transcend the mind that deceives and divides you, and your aura shines like a "golden lingam."

There is no waste in totality; the mind is the process of thought absent from meditation. Being is infinite, without image and without thought process.

You can transform all your acts into meditation, and meditation itself will transcend acts. Meditation is no-mind (meditate). It is above desires, yet feels no superiority, but REMAINS ALERT, because if you think you have no DESIRE you are already in non-meditative mind. This is very subtle and inexpressible. Only in duality does one try to be above the one as if it were "another," which is why a hypnotic dream of victims and victimizers appears, although reality is already there, abiding forever. When there is a struggle, you cancel out the observer. You can become the observer with no need for antagonism against what you observe, and without any inclinations.

You can observe your thoughts:

- ❖ By letting them circulate
- ❖ Without judging them
- ❖ Without cataloging them
- ❖ Without identifying yourself

Become the indifferent observer of your mind, and you will see that the only thing that changes incessantly is your thinking and your egoic feeling. What endures (does not change).

"Realize" now for the first time that if you think you need that change, you are just scratching the surface, because soon another change will come, and another and another. And all these changes pertain to transience and have nothing to do with transformation.

So, simply BE AWARE that you can become the observer of your own changing mental drama, in your head, and that in reality it is not you.

If you attain conscious consciousness, your transformation begins in transmutation, until the final metamorphosis from which there is no return.

Only CONSCIOUSNESS connecting, manifested transience with the core of being means becoming aware of what is real. Before becoming conscious of ideology, doctrinal dogma and the market impose a ceiling upon the individual in question. When we see that consciousness is the eternal present and the substrate underlying totality, we must recognize it as the heartbeat of the soul here/now. Only the plane of pure consciousness expresses the absolute oneness of being and its divinity.

Being aware that you can become the observer makes you discover that every event is casual, and your mental interpretation of events is not the event itself, but simply your distorted dual need. With this recognition your universal intelligence is activating and your mind deactivating, because the only thing that matters in the cosmic game is the seer of the change, not the change seen. If you merge into the seer, then the seen and the change become irrelevant.

Only the seer of the change discovers what changes, without identifying emotionally with what is changing.

Thoughts and thinkers, theses and theories, doctrines and ideologies, isms and beliefs of all kinds will appear again and again in the world, that "forest of words." In fact, each mentality creates its own world, and each conceptualization is accompanied by dual judgments about it, because whoever identifies with the changing world tends to comment on what has already happened as fact. And at most all they can do is project "the war of ideas" onto a dead event.

You will need to grasp your observer, without subject (mind) and without object (matter) because "they are two." And if that happens, the observer has freed itself of any concept.

As you become aware of the void, the world itself will continue to change. Where the mind, desire, and change (SAMSARA) come to an end, there begins conscious consciousness (NIRVANA), which has never been limited. NIRVANA is the state of the consciousness liberated from its being, with no sensory deception, no dual mind, and no attachment to name and form.

These are two apparent attitudes:

❖ In SAMSARA you identify with names and forms

❖ In NIRVANA you discover your own identity, leading to absolute bliss without the need for external stimuli

...Because all the veils have already been burned. That blessed bliss is what you are, and it has always been there. When your entire mountaintop was of the ego, you were asleep in consciousness. The ego was limited to elevating itself, climbing a mountain, as if it were "a separate island." This game does NOT PERCEIVE that the differences in the phenomenological world are only mental distortions, because it is itself the protagonist of such distorted differences.

When you stop burdening the personal leading role with distorted differences you can become a brilliant actor with no identification with the role; then the stage never touches you, because it is only about the play, and as you play and play the stage itself disappears.

The true actor and the brilliance of his soul never react to the social structure, which changes and transits. The brilliant actor is neither for or against anything, because if everything is in transit everything will pass, and the goal of life is the very moment of consciousness. The actor is not taking anything personally, for each moment is new, young and bright. It's not serious, it's just a role, a part in the play, a harmless and spontaneous performance. He has recognized that HE IS ONLY AN INSTRUMENT. The brilliant actor has also realized that society is not separated from the divine essence, and says only "blessed be," because the supreme is simultaneously absolute and relative; consciousness is here, the light of the spontaneous instant, with no separation, where the mind lacks for nothing. If you have merged with the moment itself, always new, without prior actions mattering or defining you,

You are conscious.

Only in such totality does one appear as oneness with no counterpart; it was only in the eyes of the mind that reality had seemed divided.

The truth is that reality is a whole and not a fragment; being is divinity now and forever. From the perspective of totality, everything is being.

Accept the whole as one, and that deep acceptance becomes your total relaxation, free of any fragmented and distorted mental conceptualization. Nothing is separate; all ignorance is no more than an enormous differentiation, which does not accept life as it is presented as a result of impressions in memory and conditioning. Struggle was born in the mind that looks at the world as an enemy. If the ego looks at the world as an enemy, how could it rid itself of it without trying to defeat it?

Beyond mental duality, it becomes apparent that God never failed, because God has always been and will always be omnipresent oneness.

When you attain conscious consciousness, you have seen that you can reach Nirvana only by becoming free of desire, because desire is the thief of your joy and your present, the unnatural opponent of your spontaneity. Desire is the favorite ally of interest, and promotes temporal relationships in the mind. Desire seeks to bring into this moment that which is not manifesting. To be free from desire is the supreme state of purity. The renunciation of desire is heaven itself.

Desire arises from the tendency of the mind to compare itself, believing that it needs to be completed in the individual or image, with no identity of its own, and identified with transience. An identified person, being disturbed by desire, cannot develop humanity because they only intend to achieve the object of their desire. Remember that neither in business nor in politics can you truly flow with life. The market itself is just one strategy after another, because it consists only in struggling and competing for gain; as for politics, it is a structure that exists to safeguard created interests of an economic and social nature, whether created now or in the future.

This does not in the least affect reality, which is unchanging. If you think always of the supreme lord, your heart will become pure. If the mind becomes enlightened, all worldly thoughts are subjugated.

> BEING means to be centered in ONENESS
> now and forever,
> discarding the doings of the mind
> linked to its needs,
> its interests and its undertakings.

Being is impossible on the basis of the mind. You can be spontaneous only if you do not act from the mind.

Recognizing that you are not the doer or maker of the mind constitutes surrender to the center of your being; and the courage to accept that you are merely an instrument in the hands of the supreme lord vanquishes the mortal fear of death.

If your life consists of stress and effort, you will look at death with terror; but if you look at life as a wave, death is merely the ocean; and if you have grasped the ocean, you will never again be interested in becoming the wave, which at last becomes the foam. From that point of view, death is simply relaxation, the final victory over the life that your ego-mind has fabricated. A return to the source, knowing that everything created will die.

Never fool yourself again.

The thought process cannot be your center. However brilliant it may seem, no thought is real because it does not endure. Thus, what you once called time is only the duration of a thought. The real is atemporal.

You can think about death, but this does not mean dying; and you can exist without thinking, without being born, and without dying.

The ego lacks the psychological freedom to inquire for itself. The ego attempts to tolerate fear, but cannot resolve it because fear creates false expectation and false roles; in fact, all your expectations dwell in your mind as a subtle challenge, seeking to project your desire in "time."

"THE FALSEHOOD IN THE HEAD"

If what is real is repressed within you and the unreal has been imposed on you as if it were the real, all of the needs in your "head" are false; and if your needs are false, how could you satisfy them?

If your morality is embellished and conditioned, the only thing that is guaranteed is your hypocrisy. If you talk about unity with your family but are selfish, it is hypocrisy. If a rational world has been imposed on you, whose responsibility is it but yours? Carrying such an imposition you can't face existence starting from the reasonless heart.

You may have noticed that waiting and hoping constitutes the longest chapter of your life; but it never ends and you never really enjoy it, because if you are waiting you never experience the present moment of life in a natural way.

The whole Drama is in itself merely a projection of name and form onto the stage of temporality. Now you can learn, once and for all, that the mind is a useful, secondary instrument. A focus device for temporary use that relies on words, not realities.

The mind produces the dual phenomenon of comparison and identification with reflections. Everyone who gets caught in phenomenological reflections is lost in reality. And if your mind is your master, your body will become the slave of your desire.

We say that you are on a mental trip when any emotional wave disturbs you, disperses and puts you out of focus. You know that you are in your true center, when nothing and nobody disturbs you or puts you off-center. You know that you are engaged with the mind when you choose the convenient direction of the ego even when you perceive that it is not right.

This directional electivity only happens if your mind is conditioned. You know that you have grasped what is real when you can accept the void, opening the door of the imageless infinite. The falsehood of the head is linked to appearance (what it seems to be); a relative world is a world of appearance accessed by the conditioned "I" through the limited sensory senses because they simulate states. You cannot access the real through the senses.

The only thing that is not illusion is being, because being is the seer. The body is the seen. Being sees the movement of the mind and can be an unaffected witness of all that is apparent without separating itself from it, thus turning the whole universe into beauty, harmony, celebration and grace.

Just be the observer of what changes and transits. In this play called life, if you identify with temporality you limit yourself; if you become attached to objects, you will be stultified.

If you really want to understand the joke of temporality, convince yourself that by looking "outside" you will not find the real thing. As long as you believe you have a beginning and an end, you will be confined between birth and death. This is unfortunate, because you are confusing appearances for reality. What you believe yourself to be is in fact nothing more than your ego-trajectory, and you believe that you are "this" because you are sleeping in the world of appearances. But your "ego-trajectory" is also your timeworn mind carrying open mental wounds. If you dare right now, in this moment, to let go of the "timeworn mind," you can renew yourself, and put an end to the falsehood in your head.

> "I" and "something"
> "I" and "mine" is illusion, tied to name and form, with interest and a possessive temperament (timeworn mind)
> "I" without "something" is eternity itself.
> "I" and "something" are absent in meditation.
> "I" without "something" encompasses meditation.
> "I" and "something" needs attachment to the body.
> "I" without "something" has no attachment at all.
> "I" and "something" are identification, the limit.
> "I" without "something" is the I without a self, with no fear of non-support.

All your immortal mental fear is your separation. If you develop permanent conscious alertness, the uncertainty disappears.

Fear is the emotion appropriate to the mind that looks at two sides, because you have not recognized your infinite and divine center, full of unconditional and selfless love. This is the falsehood in your head that you can release right now, because it has only to do with the finite and the material. Where your fear ends, your courage begins or the strength of virtue. Where your mind ends, consciousness or vision of oneness as oneness with everything begins.

If fear fights against fear, panic arises.
Once you know that there is an indestructible infinite center, an unfathomable void,

YOU ARE NOT THERE.

The big screen of the world no longer has anything to show your intellect, for you have taken refuge. You have merged with the indivisible, free of conceptualism. If you are fused into the indivisible, why would you need to defeat the intellect? It is no longer embellished; you are the underlying substrate, with no separation, refraction, or rejection. You have fully recognized that no thought is necessary; you have seen that no non-existent past can touch you. You don't need anyone's opinions about anything at all, you don't need authorization or approval; you are simply not separated from anything - there is no other, seen as separate, to be reflected by; indeed, you have come to comprehend

THE VOID.

RIGHT NOW

Your internal silence is infinite; there is no more belief that you are in silence. There is SAMADHI, the union of BUDHI with BRAHMAN, of the intellect with the INDIVISIBLE BEING that we are.

What was called MIND could be torn down because it needed the past, duality and desire to subsist and create appearances; it contradicted itself and confused you, because it identified with changes that it itself generated.

What was called ego could then disappear. By enlightening yourself, without thought, you see yourself as a witness who does not seek to change anything; always simply loving and serving. Always contemplating being.

That infinite vibration is stillness without image, without mirror, without individualism. In the direct vision you have been crowned for always.

THE SI-LENCE.

The 9 Steps of Internal Purpose to help Love Blossom

Step 1
The Decision to Walk

Step 2
The Vibrational Rhythmic
Fortress in the Path

Step 3
Mental Resolve in
Consciousness

Step 4
Having no attachment to the Vehicular Role

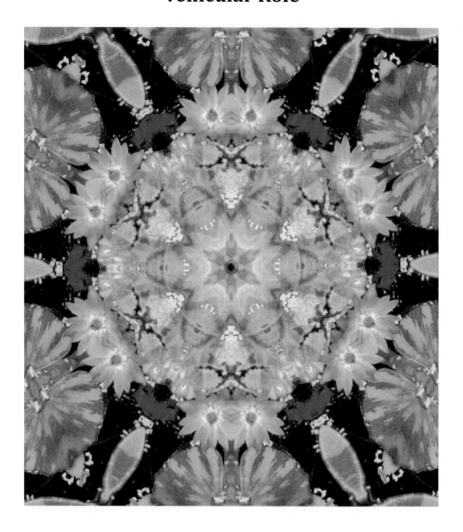

Step 5
Living Fluidly and Free of
Emotional Affectation

Step 6
Indifference to Criticism, Praise or Fame

Step 7
Being Connected to Atma

Step 8
Transcending the Illusory Duality
of Imaginary Opposites

Step 9
Live the Moment, without Private Mental Goals, that Frame an Expectation, provoking the Illusion of a Personal Disappointment

YOGA BUDHI
TAKING REFUGE

THE ART OF STAYING
YOUNG FOREVER

AT HIS DIVINE LOTUS FEET

Table of Contents

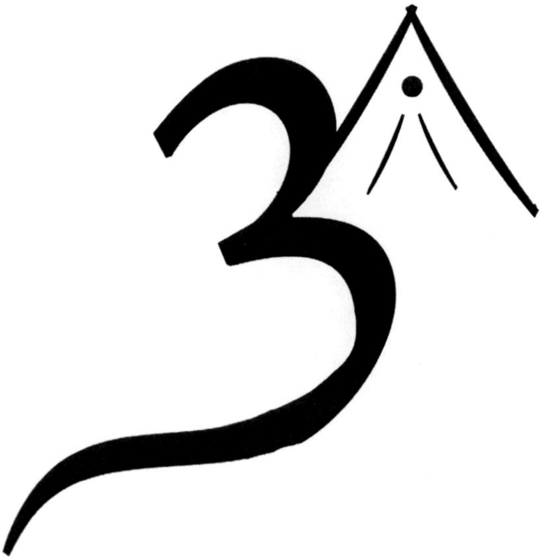